Phoenix
MERCURY

by Luke Hanlon

Copyright © 2026 by Press Room Editions. All rights reserved. No part of this book may be used or reproduced in any manner whatsoever, including internet usage, without written permission from the copyright owner, except in the case of brief quotations embodied in critical articles and reviews.

Book design by Kate Liestman
Cover design by Kate Liestman

Photographs ©: Melissa Tamez/Icon Sportswire/AP Images, cover; Chris Coduto/Getty Images Sport/Getty Images, 4, 7, 8; Harry How/Allsport/Getty Images Sport/Getty Images, 10; Todd Warshaw/Getty Images Sport/Getty Images, 13; Scott Troyanos/Allsport/Getty Images Sport/Getty Images, 14; Will Powers/AP Images, 16; Gregory Shamus/Getty Images Sport/Getty Images, 19, 20; Christian Petersen/Getty Images Sport/Getty Images, 22; Leon Bennett/Getty Images Sport/Getty Images, 25; Ross D. Franklin/AP Images, 27; Andy Lyons/Getty Images Sport/Getty Images, 29

Press Box Books, an imprint of Press Room Editions.

ISBN
979-8-89469-018-6 (library bound)
979-8-89469-031-5 (paperback)
979-8-89469-056-8 (epub)
979-8-89469-044-5 (hosted ebook)

Library of Congress Control Number: 2025932103

Distributed by North Star Editions, Inc.
2297 Waters Drive
Mendota Heights, MN 55120
www.northstareditions.com

Printed in the United States of America
082025

ABOUT THE AUTHOR

Luke Hanlon is a sportswriter and editor based in Minneapolis. He's written dozens of nonfiction sports books for kids and spends a lot of his free time watching his favorite Minnesota sports teams.

TABLE of CONTENTS

CHAPTER 1
CEMENTING A LEGACY 5

CHAPTER 2
HEATING UP 11

CHAPTER 3
SOARING IN PHOENIX 17

CHAPTER 4
ADDING TALENT 23

SUPERSTAR PROFILE
DIANA TAURASI 28

QUICK STATS 30
GLOSSARY 31
TO LEARN MORE 32
INDEX 32

CHAPTER 1

CEMENTING A LEGACY

Diana Taurasi looked for an opening. The shot clock was winding down. But the veteran Phoenix Mercury guard didn't panic. Taurasi dribbled to her right. Then she stepped back. Taurasi unloaded a long jumper. The shot clock buzzer sounded as the ball fell through the hoop.

Diana Taurasi averaged 16 points per game during the 2023 season.

At 41 years old, Taurasi had made hundreds of three-pointers during her Women's National Basketball Association (WNBA) career. This one put her close to history, though. Coming into a 2023 game against the Atlanta Dream, Taurasi needed 18 points to reach 10,000 career points. No other WNBA player had ever come close to that number. Taurasi wanted to reach that mark in front of her home fans.

Taurasi's deep shot gave her 15 points in the game. Everyone in Phoenix's arena knew she was three points away from history. On the next Mercury possession, Taurasi's teammates worked to get her the ball.

Taurasi shoots over two Atlanta defenders during a 2023 game.

Taurasi stood in the right corner of the court. Phoenix forward Brianna Turner ran over to set a screen. Taurasi's defender avoided it. Then another Atlanta defender ran to guard Taurasi as well. The Dream tried everything to stop her. But Taurasi

7

Taurasi celebrates scoring 10,000 career points in the WNBA.

didn't pass the ball. With two defenders near her, she put up a three-pointer. The ball hit nothing but net.

Taurasi's teammates ran toward her. They huddled around Taurasi and jumped up and down. The referees stopped the game to allow the celebration. The home fans went wild for their historic star scorer.

The celebrations didn't throw off Taurasi. When the game restarted, the Mercury still ran their offense through her. She continued to score easily. Taurasi finished the game with 42 points. The Mercury won 91–71. Even in her 40s, Taurasi could still score with ease. And Phoenix fans couldn't get enough of watching her.

LONG TIME COMING

Scoring 40 points in a game was nothing new for Diana Taurasi. She first reached that number during a game in July 2006. However, her 42-point outburst against the Dream came out of nowhere. Before that game, Taurasi hadn't recorded a 40-point game in 13 years.

CHAPTER 2

HEATING UP

The history of the Phoenix Mercury dates back to the beginning of the WNBA. In 1997, Phoenix became one of the league's original eight teams. Before their first season started, the Mercury hired a legend to run the team.

Phoenix brought in Cheryl Miller as the coach and general manager.

Umeki Webb (21) played for the Mercury for two seasons.

Miller was already in the Basketball Hall of Fame for her playing career. The Mercury hoped she could coach as well as she'd played.

CAREER CUT SHORT

Cheryl Miller once scored 105 points in a high school game. She then starred at the University of Southern California. She led the Trojans to two national titles. After that, Miller helped the US women's Olympic team win gold in 1984. However, she never played in the WNBA. Knee injuries ended her playing career in the late 1980s.

Miller led the Mercury to success right away. Phoenix played tough defense. Guard Michele Timms racked up steals. The Mercury ran their offense through forward Jennifer Gillom. This duo helped Phoenix make the playoffs in 1997.

Michele Timms (left) averaged 2.6 steals per game in 1997.

But the New York Liberty defeated the Mercury to end their season.

Phoenix came back even stronger in 1998. Gillom averaged 20.9 points. She led the team back to the playoffs. In the semifinals, the Mercury defeated

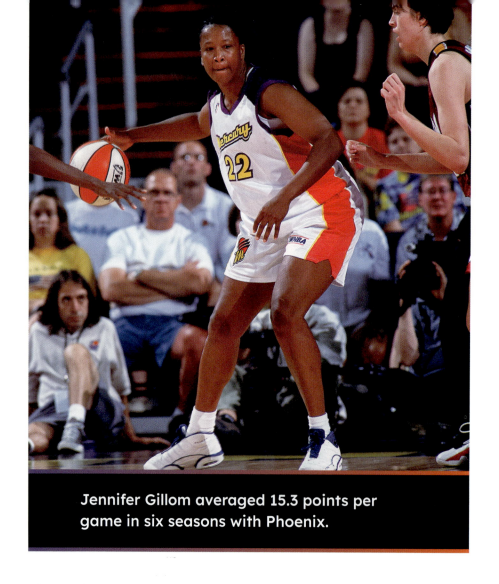
Jennifer Gillom averaged 15.3 points per game in six seasons with Phoenix.

the Cleveland Rockers. That set up a WNBA Finals matchup against the Houston Comets.

The Comets were the defending champions. They had lost only three games all season. But the Mercury stunned the Comets and won Game 1 in Phoenix. Then the best-of-three series moved to Houston. The home crowd lifted the Comets. They won both games to defend their title.

The loss stung. But Miller kept the Mercury competitive. In 2000, Phoenix won a team-record 20 games. However, the Los Angeles Sparks swept the Mercury out of the playoffs. After the season, Miller stepped down as the team's coach.

The Mercury began to struggle without Miller. Losing seasons became a routine. In 2003, the Mercury posted the worst record in the league. But that ended up helping the team's future.

CHAPTER 3

SOARING IN PHOENIX

The Mercury's bad record in 2003 helped them get the top pick in the 2004 draft. Phoenix used that pick on Diana Taurasi. The guard had starred at the University of Connecticut. She led the Huskies to three straight national titles. The Mercury hoped Taurasi could help bring a championship to Phoenix.

Diana Taurasi (3) made the All-WNBA First Team in 2004.

Taurasi quickly proved she could handle the WNBA. She averaged 17 points per game in 2004. Her scoring earned her the WNBA Rookie of the Year Award. With Taurasi leading the way, the Mercury steadily improved. In Taurasi's first two seasons, the team barely missed the playoffs.

Phoenix made a big move before the 2006 season. The team hired Paul Westhead as its new head coach. He had been coaching since the 1970s. And Westhead always wanted his teams to play fast. The goal of his offense was to shoot in seven seconds or less. He brought this same strategy to the Mercury.

Cappie Pondexter made three All-Star teams in four seasons with Phoenix.

Under Westhead, Taurasi led the WNBA in scoring in 2006. The Mercury had the league's best offense. But they missed

In 2007, Penny Taylor scored 20 or more points in four different playoff games.

the playoffs again. That changed in 2007. Finally, the team fully clicked. The Mercury finished with the best record in their conference. Then they won four straight playoff games to reach the Finals.

Phoenix faced the defending champion Detroit Shock. The Shock won two of the first three games in the best-of-five series. Guard Cappie Pondexter kept the Mercury alive in Game 4. Late in the fourth quarter, she hit a shot to seal a 77–76 win. Forward Penny Taylor then scored 30 points in Game 5. For the first time, the Mercury were WNBA champions!

SERIAL WINNER

Paul Westhead's first season as a National Basketball Association (NBA) coach came in 1979–80. That year, he led the Los Angeles Lakers to a championship. He made history when he coached the Mercury to a title 27 years later. Westhead became the first coach to win NBA and WNBA titles.

CHAPTER 4

ADDING TALENT

Paul Westhead left the Mercury after the 2007 season. Corey Gaines took over. He had been one of Westhead's assistants. So, Phoenix's offense didn't slow down. By 2009, the Mercury were back in the Finals.

The Indiana Fever took a 2–1 lead in the series. But the Mercury battled back. Diana Taurasi led the way in

Taurasi won the WNBA Most Valuable Player (MVP) Award in 2009.

Game 5 with 26 points. She lifted Phoenix to another title.

The Mercury were contenders every year with Taurasi. However, she suffered an injury early in the 2012 season. Without their star, the Mercury crumbled. They won only seven games.

Phoenix bounced back quickly. The team had the top pick in the 2013 draft. The Mercury used it on 6-foot-9 (206-cm) center Brittney Griner. Opponents had to be careful in the paint against the Mercury. Griner often waited near the basket to block shots.

The Mercury dominated in 2014 under new head coach Sandy Brondello. Griner led a great defense. And Taurasi powered

Brittney Griner (42) won the WNBA Defensive Player of the Year Award in 2014 and 2015.

the offense. The Mercury lost only one playoff game on their way to the Finals. Once they got there, the Chicago Sky didn't stand a chance. The Mercury swept the Sky to secure another title.

Brondello kept the team humming for years. Starting in 2015, the Mercury made it to the semifinals for four straight years. However, they lost each time. The team broke through in 2021. Griner had her best season yet. She led the Mercury to the Finals. Unfortunately for Mercury fans, the Chicago Sky won in four games.

Taurasi played through the 2024 season. She spoke to the Phoenix

NEW SCORER

Kahleah Copper played against the Mercury in the 2021 Finals. She earned Finals MVP honors and helped the Chicago Sky win the title. By 2023, she had made three straight All-Star Games. After that season, Phoenix traded multiple players and draft picks for Copper. She fit in right away with the Mercury. In 2024, she led Phoenix with 21.1 points per game.

Taurasi gets emotional while addressing the Phoenix crowd after the final home game of the 2024 season.

crowd after the last home game of the season. Now 42, Taurasi didn't say if she would retire or not. The home fans chanted, "One more year!" They weren't ready to stop watching the best player in team history.

SUPERSTAR PROFILE

DIANA TAURASI

Before the 2004 draft, everyone knew Diana Taurasi would be the top pick. Scouts thought she was the perfect WNBA prospect. Taurasi entered the league with high expectations. Even so, she more than lived up to the hype.

Scoring always came easy for Taurasi. She could get hot from three-point range at any moment. And she could create her own shot almost anywhere on the court. Those skills led her to five WNBA scoring titles. In 2017, Taurasi passed Tina Thompson as the WNBA's all-time leading scorer. Thompson scored 7,488 points in 496 games. Taurasi passed that mark in only 377 games.

Taurasi's scoring ability led to tons of wins. She helped the Mercury reach the playoffs 14 times. And she played a key role in the team's three championships. In 2009 and 2014, Taurasi earned Finals MVP honors.

Taurasi averaged more than 20 points per game in seven different seasons with the Mercury.

QUICK STATS

PHOENIX MERCURY

Founded: 1997

Championships: 3 (2007, 2009, 2014)

Key coaches:
- Paul Westhead (2006–07): 41–27, 7–2 playoffs, 1 WNBA title
- Corey Gaines (2008–13): 90–101, 11–9 playoffs, 1 WNBA title
- Sandy Brondello (2014–21): 150–108, 24–19 playoffs, 1 WNBA title

Most career points: Diana Taurasi (10,646)

Most career assists: Diana Taurasi (2,394)

Most career rebounds: Brittney Griner (2,322)

Most career blocks: Brittney Griner (812)

Most career steals: Diana Taurasi (518)

Stats are accurate through the 2024 season.

GLOSSARY

conference
A smaller group of teams that make up part of a sports league.

draft
An event that allows teams to choose new players coming into the league.

general manager
The person in a team's front office who drafts and signs new players.

paint
The area between the basket and the free-throw line.

prospect
A player who people expect to do well at a higher level.

rookie
A first-year player.

scouts
People who look for talented young players.

screen
When an offensive player blocks a defender to create space for a teammate.

swept
Won all the games in a series.

veteran
A player who has spent several years in a league.

TO LEARN MORE

Gerstner, Joanne C. *Diana Taurasi*. Focus Readers, 2022.

O'Neal, Ciara. *The WNBA Finals*. Apex Editions, 2023.

Whiting, Jim. *The Story of the Phoenix Mercury*. Creative Education, 2024.

MORE INFORMATION

To learn more about the Phoenix Mercury, go to **pressboxbooks.com/AllAccess**. These links are routinely monitored and updated to provide the most current information available.

INDEX

Atlanta Dream, 6–7, 9

Brondello, Sandy, 24, 26

Chicago Sky, 25–26
Cleveland Rockers, 14
Copper, Kahleah, 26

Detroit Shock, 21

Gaines, Corey, 23
Gillom, Jennifer, 12–13
Griner, Brittney, 24, 26

Houston Comets, 14–15

Indiana Fever, 23

Los Angeles Sparks, 15

Miller, Cheryl, 11–12, 15

New York Liberty, 13

Pondexter, Cappie, 21

Taurasi, Diana, 5–9, 17–19, 23–27, 28
Taylor, Penny, 21
Thompson, Tina, 28
Timms, Michele, 12
Turner, Brianna, 7

Westhead, Paul, 18–19, 21, 23